—The letter "p" photograph by Gretchen Dow Simpson

—The artwork for the letter "l" is reproduced with permission from the Block Island Southeast Lighthouse Foundation.

—The artworks that illustrate the letters c, d, f, o, r and w, and the cover of the book, were taken from paintings that originally appeared on covers of *The New Yorker* magazine. They are reprinted here by special permission of *The New Yorker* magazine and all rights are reserved. © 1976, 1977, 1988, 1989 and 1990 *The New Yorker* magazine, Inc.

Gretchen's abc
Copyright © 1991 by Gretchen Dow Simpson
Printed in the U.S.A. All rights reserved.
Typography by Al Cetta
1 2 3 4 5 6 7 8 9 10
First Edition

Library of Congress Cataloging-in-Publication Data
Simpson, Gretchen Dow.
  Gretchen's abc/by Gretchen Dow Simpson.
    p.   cm.
  "A Laura Geringer book."
  Summary: Elegant paintings illustrate each letter of the alphabet.
  ISBN 0-06-025645-1. — ISBN 0-06-025646-X (lib. bdg.)
  1. English language — Alphabet — Juvenile literature.
[1. Alphabet.]   I. Title.
PE1155.S55   1991   90-19332
[E]—dc20   CIP
                                          AC

This book is dedicated, with love and admiration,
to my favorite children, Phoebe and Megan.

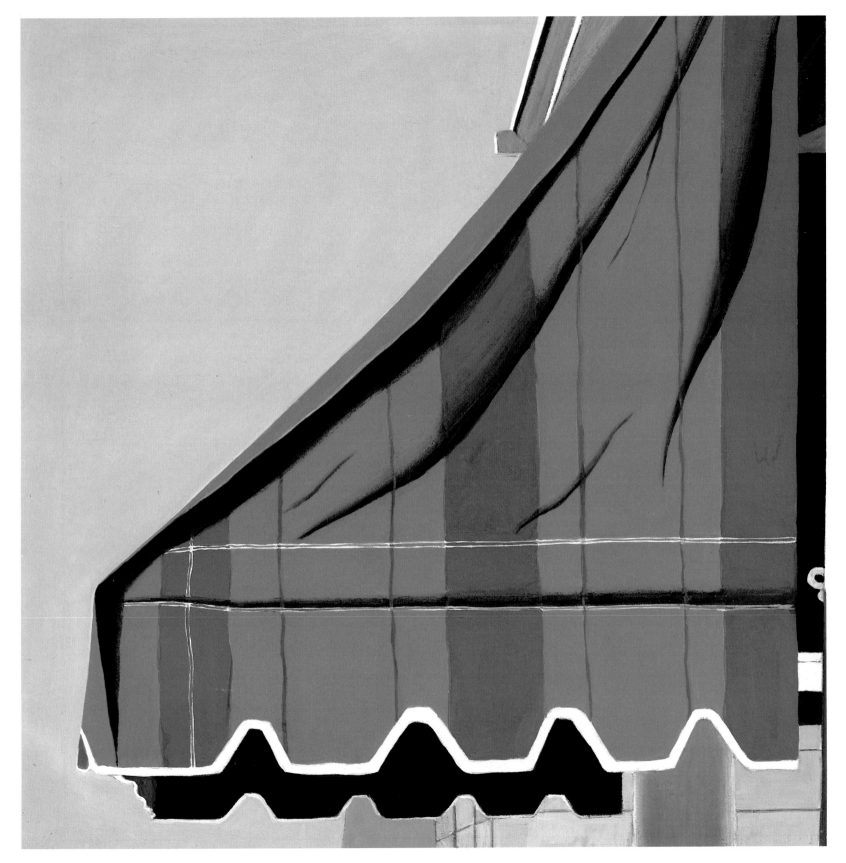

a

b

C

d

e

f

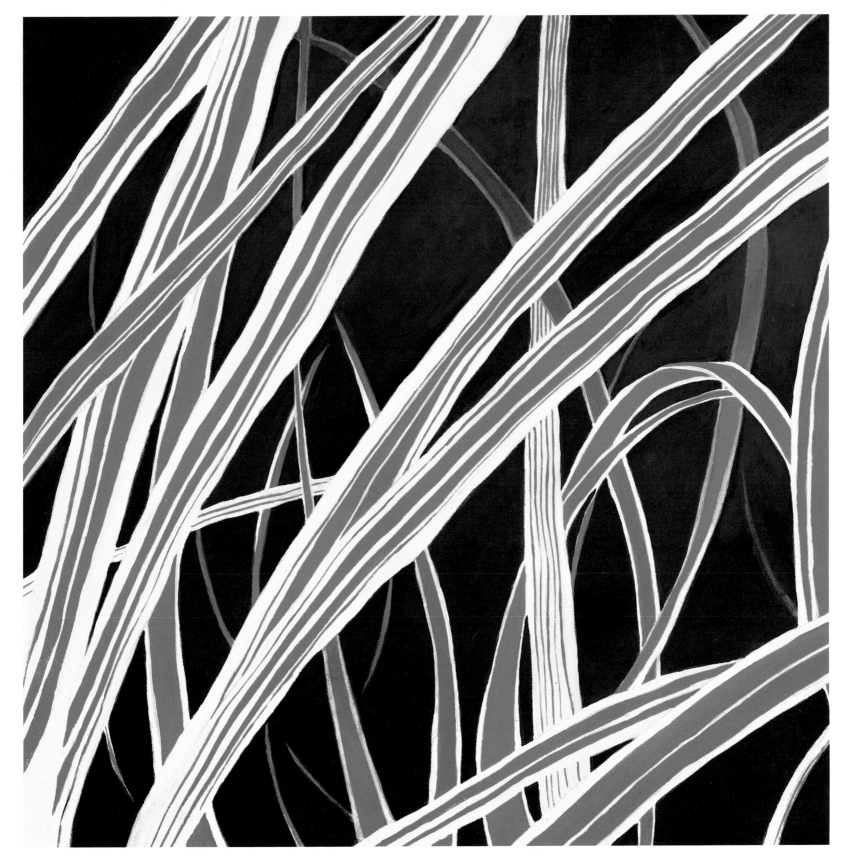

g

h

i

j

k

1

m

n

O

p

q

r

S

t

u

V

W

X

y

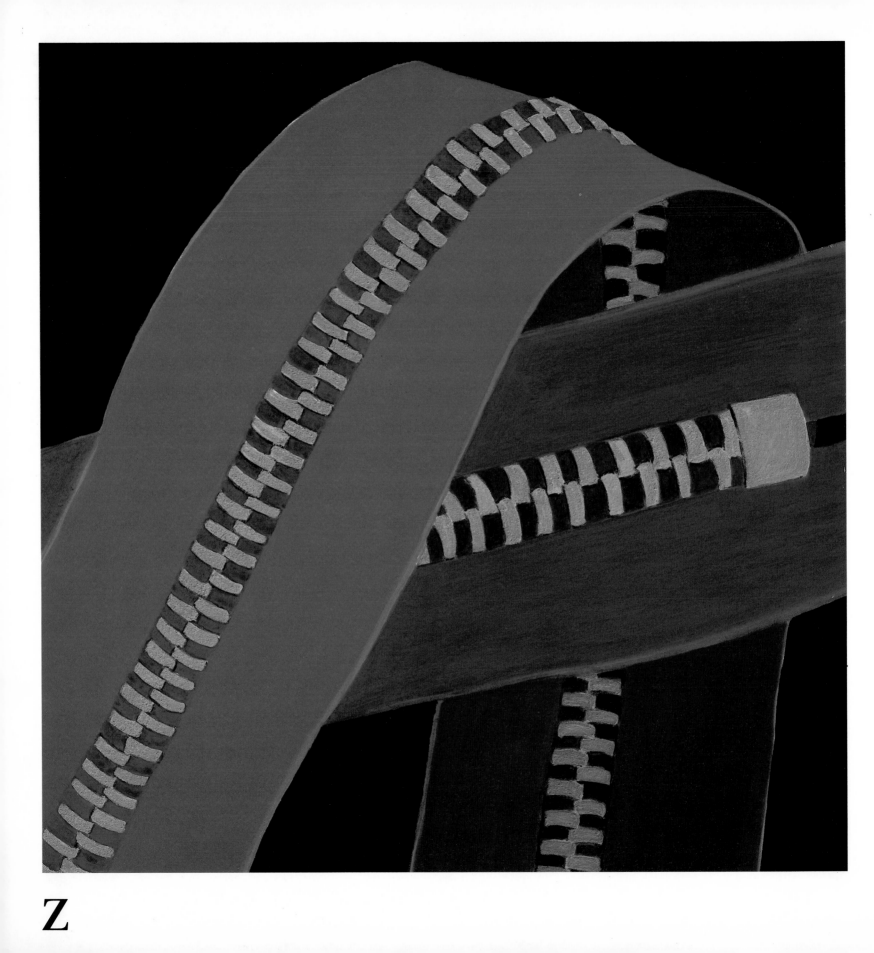

z

Gretchen's abc

a	awning	n	nails
b	bench	o	oranges
c	cabbages	p	photograph
d	dance shoes	q	quilt
e	eggs	r	rowboats
f	flags	s	stairs
g	grass	t	train tracks
h	hose	u	unicycle
i	iris	v	vine
j	jars	w	window
k	kiwifruit	x	xylophone
l	lighthouse	y	yard
m	marbles	z	zippers